This Christmas Coloring Book
Belongs To:

____

____

Date: _______/___/____

Write and Draw to Express Yourself

Date: ___ / ___ / ___

Write and Draw to Express Yourself

Date: _______ / ___ / ___

Write and Draw to Express Yourself

Date: ___ / ___ / ___

Write and Draw to Express Yourself

Date: ___/___/___

Write and Draw to Express Yourself

Date: ___/___/___

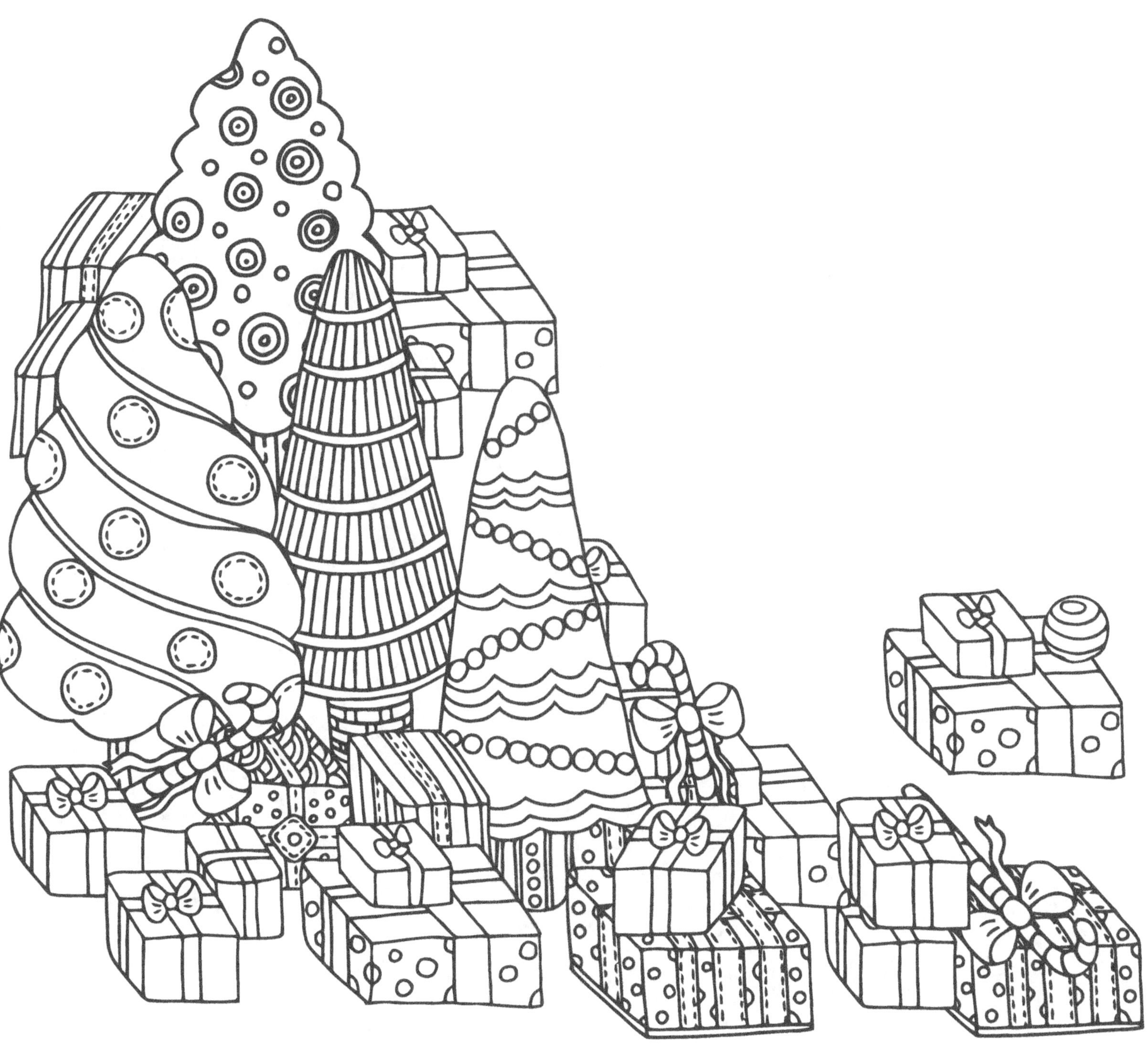

Write and Draw to Express Yourself

Date: _____ / / _____

Date: _____ / ___ / ______

Write and Draw to Express Yourself

Date: ___/___/___

Date: _____ / _____ / _____

Write and Draw to Express Yourself

Date:
xmas

Write and Draw to Express Yourself

Date:

Date: ____/____/____

Write and Draw to Express Yourself

Date: _____ / ___ / ___

Write and Draw to Express Yourself

Christmas Time

Date: ______ / ___ / ______

Write and Draw to Express Yourself

Date: ___ / ___ / ___

Write and Draw to Express Yourself

Write and Draw to Express Yourself

Date: ___ / ___ / ___

Date: ______ / ______ / ______

Write and Draw to Express Yourself

Date: ___/___/___

Merry Christmas

Write and Draw to Express Yourself

Date: ___/___/___

Write and Draw to Express Yourself

Date: _____ / / _____

Date: _______ / _______ / _______

Write and Draw to Express Yourself

Date: _______ / ____ / ________

Write and Draw to Express Yourself

Date: ___/___/___

Write and Draw to Express Yourself

Date: ___ / ___ / ___

Write and Draw to Express Yourself

Date:

Write and Draw to Express Yourself

Date: _______/____/_______

Write and Draw to Express Yourself

Date: ___/___/___

Write and Draw to Express Yourself

The Magic of Christmas

Write and Draw to Express Yourself

Write and Draw to Express Yourself

Date: ___/___/___

Write and Draw to Express Yourself

Write and Draw to Express Yourself

Write and Draw to Express Yourself

Date: ___/___/___

Write and Draw to Express Yourself

Date: ___ / ___ / ___

Write and Draw to Express Yourself

Date:

Date: ___/___/___

Write and Draw to Express Yourself

Write and Draw to Express Yourself

Date: ____/____/____

Write and Draw to Express Yourself

peace
&
joy

Write and Draw to Express Yourself

Date: /   /

Date: ___/___/___

Write and Draw to Express Yourself

Date: ___/___/___

Date: ______/______/______

Write and Draw to Express Yourself

Date: ___ / ___ / ___

Write and Draw to Express Yourself

Date: ___ / ___ / ___

Write and Draw to Express Yourself

Date: _____ / ___ / _____

Write and Draw to Express Yourself

Date: _____/_____/_____

Date: _______ / _______ / _______

Write and Draw to Express Yourself

Date: ___/___/___

Write and Draw to Express Yourself

Date: ___/___/___